Sally and the Sparrows

Story by Jenny Giles
Illustrations by Meredith Thomas

The sun came up
and the sparrows woke up.

"*Cheep! Cheep! Cheep!*"
said the hungry sparrows.
"*Cheep! Cheep! Cheep!*"

Sally woke up, too.

"I'm not going to stay in bed,"

she said.

"I'm going to go and see

the sparrows."

6

Sally went into the garden.

"I can see you up in the tree, little sparrows," said Sally. "Come down and see me."

The sparrows looked down
at Sally.
They stayed up in the tree.

"Are you hungry?" said Sally.

"*Cheep!*" said the sparrows.

"I'm going to get
some bread for the sparrows,"
said Sally.
"Sparrows like bread."

She ran inside.

Sally looked in the bread bin.

"Here is some bread
for the sparrows," she said,
"and here is some bread for me.
I'm hungry, too."

14

Sally sat down on the steps with the bread.

"Here you are, little sparrows," she said.

And the hungry sparrows

came down to eat with Sally.